DIGITAL TRANSFORMATION

DIGITAL TRANSFORMATION

CASSIDY SILVERWOOD

CONTENTS

Chapter 1: Introduction to the Fourth Industrial R

The Fourth Industrial Revolution represents a fundamental shift in how we live, work, and interact with the world around us. As a foundational aspect that affects many other topics around digital capabilities, we begin with a review of this revolution. The rest of this book delves into topics for consideration and debate around digital transformation. Our aim is to provide strategic discussions and insights for the boardrooms and executive offices of organizations of all sizes. These insights will challenge, inform, and support their digital ambitions and choices.

This book aims to provide insights and topics for critical thinking to help navigate the changes, providing relative or competitive advantage. It is not a guide on whether organizations may need to use technology— all organizations will need digital technology of some kind—but rather on how organizations may use it effectively and the potential stumbling blocks they can avoid. While it does not focus solely on digital strategy or information management strategy, its orientation is strategic at the highest levels of executive management. The book also addresses the implementation of digital initiatives in operational, project, and program management, where executives and leaders need insights to make informed decisions.

The majority of organizations are in the midst of digital transformation or are planning some form of digital technology implementation. Individual futures are also increasingly digital as the physical and digital worlds continue to converge. Digitalization is a significant characteristic of what has been termed the Fourth Industrial Revolution, characterized by extreme media hype and profound changes influencing our working and business lives. Understanding this emerging situation and making informed, considered decisions is crucial for our organizations and ourselves to prosper rather than flounder.

Defining the Fourth Industrial Revolution

The world is standing on the brink of a technological revolution that will fundamentally alter the way people live, work, and relate to one another. The fundamentally new nature of this revolution, along with its velocity and magnitude of change, has triggered discussions about the Fourth Industrial Revolution in many of the world's leading economies. Klaus Schwab, founder and executive chairman of the World Economic Forum, identifies "three main reasons why today's transformation represents not merely a prolongation of the Third Industrial Revolution but rather the arrival of a Fourth and distinct one: velocity, scope, and systems impact." The First Industrial Revolution used water and steam power to mechanize production. The Second used electric power to create mass production. The Third used electronics and information technology to automate production. Now, the Fourth Industrial Revolution builds on the Third, the digital revolution, which has been occurring since the middle of the last century. It is characterized by a fusion of technologies that is blurring the lines between the physical, digital, and biological spheres.

Key Technologies Driving the Fourth Industrial Revolution

In the Fourth Industrial Revolution, neither machine nor work is at the center. Instead, the focus of business enterprises shifts to building and capturing human value. Technology must focus on the customer, supporting an intimate firm-customer relationship that listens, learns, and serves, regardless of the enterprise's size. Without the ability to craft new data-driven business and revenue models and create personalized offerings in a voice that resonates with customers, firms that embrace endless signs of robotic process automation (RPA) profit growth and productivity improvement may face a revolt from their customers.

Data is the lifeblood of cognitive systems, influencing today's work environment in numerous ways. The emergence of Internet of Things (IoT) technology has been a significant catalyst driving the Fourth Industrial Revolution. This revolution promises substantial advances in the digital age, thanks to breakthroughs in artificial intelligence, cognitive systems, IoT, and new tools that allow us to navigate an increasingly data-driven and algorithm-controlled environment. However, it is crucial to remember that the Fourth Industrial Revolution is technological but also profoundly cultural. As Vanguard founder Jack Bogle said, "successful investing is about managing the relationship between reason and emotion." Transparency in data-driven decisions is essential if they are to be trusted. Rights and protections need to be consistent with risks and responsibilities. The initiative to get these values right must extend to new areas, such as responsible AI and data innovation.

This chapter sets the stage for a deeper exploration of the Fourth Industrial Revolution and its implications. In the following chapters, we will dive into various aspects of digital transformation, offering insights and strategies to navigate this complex and rapidly evolving landscape. Stay tuned for more!

Chapter 2: Understanding Digital Transformation

Introduction

Digital transformation should be regarded as a continual process of reinvention. Activities during digital acceleration that spur the reimagining of potential business models, and shift the organization's core operations, culture, and data, are integral to digital transformation. This ongoing approach, incorporating digital acceleration and continuous involvement with data, disrupts the linear nature of traditional transformation and promotes the creation of a dynamic roadmap. Such a roadmap demonstrates forward strides, generating momentum and capability that, in conjunction with continuous engagement with technology (demanding training, embedded technologies, and organizational learning), establishes an enduring presence. This presence allows organizations to navigate the digital frontier in pursuit of the paradox and promise of the Fourth Industrial Revolution.

Defining Digital Transformation

Leaders tasked with implementing digital change in their organizations often embrace the term "digital transformation." It's a buzzword that captures the unique opportunities digital offers: improving customer touchpoints, redesigning existing products and services, creating new revenue streams, and optimizing internal processes. In previous decades, consumer-facing brands developed online or mobile strategies aiming for maximum visibility, often without comprehensive business planning. Today, digitization not only enhances customer visibility but also provides valuable data and practical insights, fostering direct interactions.

Companies such as Amazon, Apple, and Google have set the benchmark, capturing our imagination and prompting an increasing number of businesses to pursue digital and data transformations. These transformations pave the way to innovation and deeper customer connections. Alongside the adoption of potent, next-generation technologies, these companies are reinventing core operational processes and entire business models. But what exactly are organizations seeking in digitization? How can companies harness its power to compete effectively in the marketplace?

Definition and Scope of Digital Transformation

The Fourth Industrial Revolution represents the intelligent, digitalized, and highly automated industry epitomized by the smart factory. This factory connects and integrates with corresponding front-end and back-end links to form an efficient industry. The Fourth Industrial Revolution has become the cornerstone and set sail of future manufacturing industry development, with its infrastructure, technology, and terminal operation services forming the core content around which global industry and the global Internet will engage in-depth cooperation and competition.

Digital transformation is the change associated with the application of digital technology in all aspects of human society. It marks a shift from an era based on hardware and software to one of business relevance, where digital technologies fundamentally change how businesses operate and deliver value to customers. In this era, business and technology are already deeply intertwined. As evidenced by significant global technological advances, digital transformation is seen as a critical engine for economic and social development.

Digital transformation has become a top priority for development in many countries. In February 2015, the Prime Minister of Germany launched the strategy "Germany. Making a reality of perfection," aiming to pursue leadership in the Fourth Industrial Revolution. In September 2017, a member of the European Parliament proposed that the European Union double its digital transformation spending within a decade.

Importance of Digital Transformation in the Fourth Industrial Revolution

Productivity improvements will not materialize unless organizations restructure to account for inherent changes in employees' roles. Implementing a clear roadmap may necessitate significant changes to an organization's structure, business model, and client value proposition. However, not every company will experience major upheaval. While technological skills have always been essential for progress, the scale is much larger today, with the rapid pace of technological change. Small and medium enterprises in the ICT sector heavily depend on digital infrastructure developments.

Organizations must invest in their business and human growth strategies. This investment includes skill acquisition and retention, ensuring a workforce of digital professionals eager to push innovation boundaries for digital growth. Digital transformation is on the strategic agenda of most organizations. The increasingly universal nature of digitally transformed business is apparent, regardless of industry and country. Most agree that digital transformation is essential for long-term survival in an already competitive and increasingly digital world. Without restructuring, introducing new technologies into existing work processes may increase efficiency, but not significantly boost productivity. Hence, organizations need a clear, long-term digital roadmap.

By expanding these ideas, we delve deeper into the nuances of digital transformation and its role in the Fourth Industrial Revolution. This added detail will help readers fully grasp the significance and breadth of digital transformation in today's world.

Chapter 3: Challenges and Opportunities in Digital

Introduction

Stakeholders often struggle to understand the necessity and objectives of digital transformation. The uncertainty surrounding how much can be digitized, how to innovate with digital technology, and how to create differentiated products or services that customers are willing to pay for remains a significant challenge. Considerations for external partners, such as distributors or clients' capabilities to accommodate digital products, are equally important.

In this context, digital transformation has emerged as a critical competitive differentiator. Organizations recognize the need to significantly enhance their digital competences, operations, and scale. We propose that digital transformation should be viewed as an organizational journey to create value through sharing, growing, and preserving. Research has highlighted key challenges associated with embarking on this journey, including forming new business/IT relationships, gaining C-suite approval for top-down digital initiatives, cross-functional alignment of resources, and fostering business recognition of the need for agility and speed in digital projects.

Challenges Faced by Organizations in Implementing Digital Transformation

Organizations face numerous challenges in their digital transformation efforts. These challenges require significant fortitude and commitment to prepare processes, infrastructure, services, and personnel to successfully navigate the Fourth Industrial Revolution. However, the necessity of transformation remains, as failing to adapt could limit an organization's competitive ability.

Common Challenges

1. **Inertia and Fear of the Unknown**: Resistance to change and fear of the unknown are common hurdles that hinder digital transformation initiatives. Organizations must address cultural resistance and foster a mindset that embraces change.
2. **Complexity**: The intricate nature of digital transformation projects, involving numerous stakeholders and technologies, adds layers of complexity that can be difficult to manage.
3. **Information Overload**: The abundance of data and information can overwhelm decision-makers, making it challenging to identify actionable insights.
4. **Uncertainty about Leveraging Technologies**: Organizations often struggle to determine which technologies to leverage and which to ignore, leading to potential misallocation of resources.
5. **Siloed Efforts**: Lack of collaboration and siloed efforts within the organization can impede the progress of digital transformation initiatives. Cross-functional alignment is crucial for success.
6. **Lack of a Clear and Unified Digital Strategy**: Without a clear and cohesive digital strategy, organizations may pursue fragmented initiatives that fail to achieve desired outcomes.

7. **Workforce Skills and Readiness Constraints**: The existing workforce may lack the necessary skills and readiness to effectively implement and manage digital technologies.
8. **Privacy and Security Concerns**: Ensuring data privacy and security in an increasingly digital environment is a significant challenge that organizations must address.

The Impact of COVID-19

The COVID-19 pandemic has introduced a new sense of urgency for digital transformation. Organizations must adapt to remote work, digital customer interactions, and new business models to remain competitive in a rapidly changing landscape. The pandemic has highlighted the importance of digital resilience and the ability to quickly pivot in response to unforeseen challenges.

Opportunities for Innovation and Growth

Despite the challenges, digital transformation offers significant opportunities for innovation, growth, and societal benefits.

Economic Diversification

Digital transformation enables economic diversification by fostering new industries and business models. It re-engages marginalized communities in the labor market and offers new employment opportunities, particularly for vulnerable individuals.

Workforce Development

The changing nature of work, driven by automation and digital technologies, creates new and emerging roles in the ICT sector. These roles have the potential to provide millions of new employment opportunities and help re-establish the middle class. Targeted training and upskilling initiatives are crucial for preparing the workforce for these new opportunities.

Inclusivity and Diversity

Digital transformation presents an opportunity to address inclusivity and diversity challenges in the workforce. Special attention should be given to educating and training women and girls whose participation in ICT education and jobs is limited. Emerging fields such as remote coding, tech support, and e-commerce offer potential for greater inclusivity and the opportunity to overcome organizational and cultural barriers.

Technological Advancements

The exponential technological advancements of the Fourth Industrial Revolution provide broader opportunities for achievements across various goals. The shift to digital computing, big data, artificial intelligence, robotization, and the Internet of Everything is transforming the production and delivery of goods and services at an unprecedented rate. These advancements present opportunities for innovation and growth, boosting the global economy, increasing productivity, and improving standards of living.

Participation in Global Markets

Small and medium-sized enterprises (SMEs), often the drivers of innovation and growth in local communities, can more easily participate in global markets through digital transformation. By leveraging digital technologies, SMEs can extract greater value from existing assets while minimizing negative environmental impacts.

This chapter outlines the key challenges and opportunities associated with digital transformation. It provides a comprehensive understanding of the obstacles organizations face and the potential benefits they can achieve by embracing digital transformation.

Chapter 4. Digital Transformation Strategies

By developing a framework of digital transformation strategies, this article contributes to the digital transformation management literature. The clarified necessity of becoming increasingly competitive and the varied application of the adaption and strategic posture leverage become influential contributors to the developed framework of digital transformation strategies. The combination of the case study and the analytical frameworks suggest that it is not only the most resourceful companies that are capable of successful digital transformation management. The company also understood that the fourth industrial revolution and digital transformation is not only a technical problem, but also the solvency of strategic targets, value network support, market disturbances management, synthesis and efficiency, and retrenchment aspects of their multilevel organization.

This article has illustrated how companies have started their journeys towards digital transformation and how they approach the learning phase. However, all the cases are also very different, as the companies are structured very differently and have designed very different strategies. Given the research design that data are collected from multiple sources and time points, this article contributes to the digital transformation literature with an understanding of how companies manage to navigate the volatile, uncertain, complex, and ambiguous world of digital transformation management and with an identification of the types of digital transformation strategies that are currently being applied. The case study on key levers of digital transformation concludes that (fashion) companies advanced in digital transformation management operate with a long-term digital transformation strategy and advanced company self-awareness. The proposed framework of the four cell opportunity portfolio could provide a probable solution by allocating the digital building blocks.

Key Components of a Successful Digital Transformation Strategy

A holistic approach to digital transformation should be fully cognizant of the following cardinal factors. Every organization needs to have clarity regarding their mission, the problem they are solving, and the impacts at multiple levels, that is, strategic, process, operational, product, and service innovation, and external. Each transformation mission needs KPIs which can be translated into business goals. These goals should be further decomposed into use cases. To support digital transformation, the digital talent of the organization should be enhanced. Data is an important enabler during the digital transformation process, and it should be on the strategic agenda so as to create a proactive place for data and intelligence in the business strategy. The transformation process should reclaim inefficient resources and secure investment by continuously tracking, adjusting, and demonstrating progress and success toward the transformation goals. Successful alignment between leadership and key change agents is necessary for implementing a successful digital transformation plan.

The components of a digital transformation strategy consist of three main interrelated areas, namely the business challenge, the use case, and the strategic response. The three are intertwined and represent the mutually dependent variables. The business challenge answers the "why" question, and this is reflected in the overall transformation ambition and mission, the opportunities, key drivers, and the challenges faced. The use case answers the "how" question, and this is reflected in the specific digital technologies most appropriate to seize the opportunity and address the challenges with an aim to realize the transformation ambition. The strategic response answers the "what" question in terms of the change management implications in three principal areas of people, process, and technology enablers. It is these sub-elements that comprise the overall strategy for transformation adoption and diffusion.

Case Studies of Effective Digital Transformation

At the heart of the digital enterprise and the core of its digital transformation is the value of data and the transformative power of advanced data analysis techniques that generate new insights and increased corporate intelligence. Organizations understand the immediate benefits of the additional productivity and efficiency that so-called data-driven technologies can deliver, particularly in areas such as cloud, artificial intelligence, machine learning, and analytics. These solutions have become business-critical, and organizations that fail to grasp their importance and capitalize on their capabilities are doomed to fail in a world that is increasingly data-driven. At the same time, organizations are also aware of the benefits that other insights, provided by a range of other technologies, can deliver. Whether through automation, monitoring, or predictive insights, these solutions can also provide the competitive advantage that organizations need. The growing value of data as a core asset makes it an increasingly tempting target for hackers and offenders. Organizations are aware of the growing risks, particularly in a situation where regulatory bodies are starting to impose severe financial penalties and other mandatory consequences for data breaches and other failures to enforce data security. This has resulted in an increasing focus on data security issues, particularly encryption, firewalls, and security scanning solutions.

There are numerous successful examples of digital transformation across sectors, and these have been the focus of in-depth case studies. This research has found that successful digital transformation is driven by a strategic intent and that the transformation process is iterative. Companies start off with early successes and expand and merge with other initiatives. This aggregation of many small moves creates an overall significant impact.

Chapter 5: Ethical and Social Implications of Digi

Introduction

Digital transformation offers vast opportunities but also requires a new mindset to address the accompanying risks. Specialists agree that this transformation will profoundly affect our identity, the values that sustain it, and the way we want to live and work. The European Commission has highlighted the need for a profound reflection on these aspects and launched a broad debate aimed at citizens to promote the ethical development and integration of digital technologies in social life, culture, economy, and institutions. The goal is to establish a European way of life that is fair and inclusive, positioning Europe as a reference point in this new era. Europe aims for products that respect basic ethical guarantees, inspired by its constitutional traditions. The European Parliament has encouraged overcoming obstacles of the digital divide and evolving democratic and institutional mechanisms to effectively control and govern the digital sphere and new technologies.

Technological advances driven by information technology and digitization are making our lives easier and more pleasant in many ways. However, as technology evolves, problems that have grown exponentially in our society are posed differently. Although technology advances, human nature remains the same, with its flaws and fears. Difficult moments, such as wars, terrorist attacks, major accidents, or pandemics, bring our values to light. We are currently experiencing an unprecedented technological avalanche that challenges even the most dystopian ideas portrayed by Hollywood. This anthropocentric shift encourages us to reflect on the social implications that new technological advances may bring about.

Privacy and Data Security Concerns

The increasing deployment of advanced technology has created an imbalance between productivity enhancements and production management imperatives. Privacy proponents and regulatory forces drive regulation to balance these interests. According to Moor, there is no action in contemporary human life that does not involve some information about a person. This creates a dilemma of permitting some disclosures while preventing others, which is difficult to resolve. In the United States, citizens have no basic right to privacy, and this startling assertion is often met with denial, rejection, and disappointment.

Privacy and data security concerns, once simmering at the margins of social consciousness, have now exploded to the forefront of public debate. High-profile e-commerce scandals, such as the Target payment breaches and K-Mart ShopYourWay credit card data breaches, have heightened awareness. Businesses are losing consumer confidence and facing backlash in the form of lawsuits to recover costs associated with fraudulent use of private information. An exponential loss in market value is also suffered by publicly traded companies targeted by cyber criminals. Statistics show that over 50% of small businesses are now being hacked, and current electronic security efforts are seen as weak. These high stakes keep cybersecurity a top enterprise issue, with all parties working together to address and ameliorate these privacy and data security concerns.

Impact on Employment and Workforce

The rise of automation and robotization significantly impacts the future workforce and its employability, reshaping the types of tasks and skills required for specific jobs. While repetitive, routine, and rule-based tasks are more vulnerable to automation, tasks requiring human-like intelligence are less susceptible. Technology, complementing rather than substituting human labor, may open up new job types and responsibilities in the industry.

Advances in genetics, neuroscience, and geriatrics, for example, pave the way for the biotech industry to diversify, allowing the workforce to adapt to new roles in computer, information technology, mathematics, life, physical, and social sciences. Workforce transformation needs to be organized in collaboration between policymakers, employers, employees, and other stakeholders. Public-private partnerships focusing on skills, diversity, adaptability, and leadership provide new collaborative platforms for dialogue and further development.

Given the flexibility and significance expected of employees, employers' and employees' needs are converging, with both wanting individuals to acquire a broad set of skills to remain employable. Addressing pressing labor market issues and matching the pool of skilled workers with market demands is crucial. Smart Industry is the accelerator driving the Fourth Industrial Revolution into the twenty-first century, offering programs and initiatives to foster skills development and workforce adaptability.

Ethical Considerations and Recommendations

Digital transformation raises significant ethical considerations. Ensuring fairness and inclusivity in digital technologies is essential. Developing ethical guidelines and frameworks to govern the use of digital technologies can help address these concerns. Policymakers, industry leaders, and society must work together to establish ethical standards that promote the responsible use of technology.

Conclusion

The ethical and social implications of digital transformation are profound. As we navigate this new era, it is essential to reflect on our values, identity, and the way we want to live and work. By addressing privacy and data security concerns, preparing the workforce for the future, and fostering ethical development, we can harness the opportunities of digital transformation while mitigating its risks. Collaborative efforts across all sectors are necessary to ensure that digital transformation benefits society as a whole.

Chapter 6: The Role of Leadership in Driving Digit

Introduction

Digital transformation impacts every aspect of an organization, from how businesses connect with customers, employees, and partners, to how internal operations are managed. At the heart of these organizational changes lies a unique digital phenomenon: the shift away from division-specific vertical hierarchies towards a connected enterprise. This connected enterprise uses digital technologies to create greater operational visibility and trust, automate key decisions, and complete customer connection chains more rapidly than ever before. This shift replaces traditional forms of process control and management with a more flexible blend of technological interconnectedness and human leadership, responsive to a world full of digital surprises.

Transformations of this scale, scope, and complexity demand more from today's organizations and involve them more closely with leadership—particularly in organizational processes, structural relationships, management practices, and decision-making styles. Leadership in the digital age is less about control and management and more about enabling quick and effective decision-making. This is achieved by institutionalizing agile organizational processes and cultivating emergent, dynamic, and creative capabilities. Digital leadership encourages a new kind of social motivation, using technology to elicit human choices and fostering an environment where innovation can thrive.

Characteristics of Effective Digital Transformation Leaders

The technology is available and occupies a position of importance within organizations. However, the real challenge lies in developing leadership capabilities that encourage collaboration among diverse, multifaceted teams. These teams must be able to mobilize resources across the organization to execute a shared vision and strategy for digital transformation at scale. Effective leaders in digital transformation, referred to as "digital transformers" and "digital alchemists," can address both the technical aspects of digital technology leadership and the softer aspects of language, collaboration, and culture.

A study of approximately 1,400 companies over a ten-year period reveals that digitally mature companies outperform their industry peers in earnings and profit margins by integrating digital technologies across their organizations. The positive correlation in earnings before interest and taxes (EBIT) and net margins has increased over the past few years, indicating that digitally mature companies manage their operations more efficiently through digital means. These companies are capable of creating new business models implemented in various ways and are not reliant on their core incumbents.

Effective digital transformation leaders exhibit the following characteristics:

1. **Visionary Thinking**: They possess a clear vision for the future of the organization and how digital technologies can be leveraged to achieve strategic goals.
2. **Agility and Adaptability**: They are able to navigate the rapidly changing digital landscape, adapting strategies and operations as needed.
3. **Collaborative Mindset**: They foster a culture of collaboration, breaking down silos and encouraging cross-functional teamwork.
4. **Empathy and Emotional Intelligence**: They understand the human side of digital transformation, recognizing and addressing the concerns and needs of employees.
5. **Innovative Spirit**: They encourage innovation, risk-taking, and creativity within the organization, recognizing and rewarding new ideas and approaches.

Building a Culture of Innovation and Adaptability

Forward-looking companies are embracing productivity tools that have transformed their operations to rethink the employee relationship. Some are rethinking management structures and practices, eliminating excessive supervisor roles and perfunctory performance-management procedures inspired by the automation of low-complexity activities. These companies are pioneering new forms of employee compensation, offering shares of profits rather than fixed pay, allowing employees to benefit from the forces of creative destruction.

A culture of innovation and adaptability is fundamental to being a digital organization. Key ingredients include:

1. **Encouraging Different Thinking**: Promoting a mindset that embraces new ideas and perspectives.

2. **Promoting a Risk-Taking Culture**: Creating an environment where taking calculated risks is encouraged and failure is viewed as a learning opportunity.
3. **Recognizing and Rewarding Innovation**: Implementing systems to acknowledge and reward innovative efforts and achievements.
4. **Removing Bureaucracy and Barriers**: Streamlining processes and eliminating unnecessary bureaucracy that stifles creativity and agility.
5. **Rethinking Employee Relationships**: As shocks to companies become more frequent, many executives recognize the need to rethink the contract with employees. This involves fostering a more flexible and responsive relationship that aligns with the dynamic nature of digital transformation.

Conclusion

Leadership plays a crucial role in driving digital transformation. Effective digital leaders possess visionary thinking, agility, a collaborative mindset, empathy, and an innovative spirit. Building a culture of innovation and adaptability is essential for organizations to thrive in the digital age. By fostering an environment that encourages different thinking, promotes risk-taking, recognizes innovation, and removes barriers, organizations can navigate the complexities of digital transformation and achieve sustained success.

Chapter 7: Measuring the Impact of Digital Transfo

Introduction

Since 2000, the ICT-capital to IT-capital (ICT-K: IT-K) ratio has declined, deviating from its cyclical patterns and raising concerns about the overestimation of Total Factor Productivity (TFP) in IT-producing industries. These industries were increasingly using their own outputs as inputs. A formal method to test for potential errors when nonlinear pricing is present and adjust the results has been developed. The TFP in ICT-producing sectors was corrected for credit-constrained high-growth firms capable of increasing ICT usage despite declining relative prices. After adjustments, with the ICT-K: IT-K ratio factored in, a higher contribution from ICT to labor productivity growth was registered, from 0.6% in 2010-12 to 0.7% in 2013-14.

In the manufacturing sector, average productivity growth rose from 0.7% in 1996-2004 to 3.6% in 2004-07, following the start of exploiting e-weights. In the five years prior to 2007, average productivity growth peaked, hitting 5.8% in 2005-07. This increase primarily reflected spillovers from IT-producing sectors and an acceleration of IT hardware power. TFP growth in general ICT-producing industries slowed from 3.9% in 2000-07 to 2.0% in 2007-09, as did IT hardware and software power growth. The measured direct contribution of ICT capital accumulation to labor productivity growth rebounded during the ICT price crash of 2002-07, peaking at 1.3 percentage points in 2003, with an average of 0.5 percentage points per year.

Key Performance Indicators for Assessing Digital Transformation Success

Assessing digital transformation success requires identifying and monitoring Key Performance Indicators (KPIs) that reflect the extent and impact of digital initiatives. These KPIs should encompass both internal and external data sources, measuring the consequences of digital adoption and the overall business operating environment.

Key Dimensions for DT KPIs:

1. **Strategic Environments**: Organizations should consider both internal and external data sources that feed potential DT KPIs relative to business operating KPIs. This includes indicators reflecting the transfer, diffusion, and scale opportunities of digital initiatives.

2. **Business Environment**: This includes factors contributing to the level of KPIs identified, such as dimensions of firms and their operations. Adopting new business models often involves transitions that need to be measured.

3. **Innovation Management**: New KPIs can be developed, or existing sets extended, to measure innovation management effectiveness specific to businesses.

Empirical Evidence for DT KPIs:

- **Profit and Loss**: The core defining property of extensive DT can be manifest in the profit and losses of adopters, requiring tools to quantify and describe.
- **Selected Metrics**: KPIs are selected metrics highlighting the overall operating situation and affecting the state of profitability of the adopting firm.

Tools and Techniques for Monitoring and Evaluation

Determining the right level of monitoring and pace of measurement is crucial for institutions undergoing digital transformation. Leaders must balance spending time and resources to monitor digital transformation activities and progress while allowing teams to enact changes.

Key Tools and Techniques:

1. **Customer Experience and Business P&L Impact**: Measure digital transformation from both customer experience and business profit and loss (P&L) impact.
2. **Digital Model**: Evaluate the overall digital model's effectiveness and its alignment with strategic goals.
3. **Cultural Impact**: Assess the impact of digital transformation on organizational culture, including employee engagement and adaptability.
4. **Business Unit Level**: Measure the impact of digital transformation at the business unit level to identify specific areas of success or needed improvement.

Systematic Monitoring and Evaluation:

- **Digital Change Assistants (DCAs)**: Utilize DCAs to understand the implications of digital transformation and manage an ecosystem network model for technology.
- **Agility and Oversight**: Ensure both agility and oversight in monitoring, capturing the right data, and making timely decisions without stifling innovation or increasing costs.
- **Small Bets for Big Conviction**: Allow for small, calculated risks that can lead to significant conviction and success in digital transformation initiatives.

Chapter 8: Future Trends in Digital Transformation

Introduction

The future of digital transformation is rapidly evolving, driven by advanced technologies and innovative applications. The complexity of these programs means they are becoming more challenging to understand, explain, and reproduce. To manage such complexity, particularly in safety-critical applications like transport, modular programming with 'open box' interfaces and trigger-fused data link systems will be necessary.

Policy responses to digital transformation waves need a strategic focus to balance economic and political opportunities created by emerging technologies such as AI and big data while managing economic and social transformation inclusively and sustainably. Minimizing the risks of the digital divide and supporting leading-edge applications, like privacy-preserving pseudo-anonymization, will be crucial in processing vast amounts of data, especially in smart city environments.

Emerging Technologies Shaping the Future of Digital Transformation

Several cutting-edge technologies are shaping the future of digital transformation, each contributing uniquely to the advancement of various industries and sectors:

Deep Learning

Deep Learning digests interpretable constructs and data patterns, enabling complex algorithms to predict results with high accuracy. Over time, the business of understanding and exploiting these manipulations of data has become more advanced and augmented, offering significant opportunities for innovation.

Machine Learning

Machine Learning (ML) is vital for interpreting massive, fast-growing datasets accurately. With AI's ability to consolidate relevant information into a single source and create predictive models that adjust as data grows, ML becomes an essential instrument in business forecasting and planning.

Artificial Intelligence (AI)

AI is the latest technological revolution with vast applications across industries, professions, and daily lives. Recognizing the profits and efficiencies of machine learning and accessing AI technologies available to most businesses today, custom AI solutions have become integral to digital transformation.

Predictions for the Evolution of Digital Transformation Practices

As digital transformation continues to evolve, several predictions can be made regarding future practices and capabilities:

General and Special Capabilities

Savvy and competencies that enhance governance and decision processes, reduce errors, and support physical and cognitive functions will be crucial. Capabilities for implementing or complementing improved digital transformation solutions from the digital transformation ecosystem will be essential.

Automatic Predicting and Adapting to Changes

Given data-like inputs and human learning processes, businesses increasingly use predictive and learning procedures as part of digital transformation. These capabilities enable automatic adaptation to changes, ensuring agility and responsiveness.

Orchestrating External and Internal Resources

Companies must be skilled at orchestrating internal and external capabilities, including pursuing digital transformation goals, enhancing AI amplification, and seeking to improve growth determinants for economic and technical roles. This includes achieving good Net Present Values (NPVs) on innovation projects or programs.

Embedding Customer or User Needs

Embedding customer or user needs into digital transformation initiatives is often overlooked but critical. This involves understanding and addressing non-technical aspects to ensure the successful adoption and integration of digital technologies.

Specifications of Specific Capabilities

Digital pilots mentor other capabilities, focusing on key assets or limits of deep value. "Peerless assets" are treasured commodities that enhance intrinsic conditions, while "irreplaceable limits" are unique, indispensable elements ensuring achievement is possible.

The fundamental digital transformation capabilities and pilot asset peculiarities predict how companies frame their digital transformation practices and architectures. Learning from the digital transformation designs and practices of exemplary companies will be revealing and contagious.

Conclusion

The future of digital transformation is marked by the continuous emergence of advanced technologies and innovative applications. Deep learning, machine learning, and artificial intelligence are driving this revolution, offering unprecedented opportunities for businesses and societies. As organizations navigate this rapidly changing landscape, they must develop and leverage specific capabilities to stay competitive and achieve sustained success.